5106

How to Draw the Life and Times of
Grover Cleveland

Betsy Dru Tecco

The Rosen Publishing Group's
PowerKids Press™
New York

To Karen and Joe Cardoni with love and laughter

Published in 2006 by The Rosen Publishing Group, Inc.
29 East 21st Street, New York, NY 10010

First Edition

Editor: Rachel O'Connor
Layout Design: Albert B. Hanner
Photo Researcher: Fernanda Rocha

Illustrations: All illustrations by Holly Cefrey.
Photo Credits: p. 4 National Portrait Gallery, Smithsonian Institution/Art Resource, NY; p. 7 © North Wind Picture Archives; p. 8 Photo by John Collins; p. 9 © Benton J. Nelson, www.presidentsgraves.com; p. 10 Library of Congress Prints and Photographs Division, Historic American Buildings Survey, NJ,7-CALD,2-2; pp. 12, 14, 16, 24 Library of Congress Prints and Photographs Division; pp. 18, 20, 26 © Corbis; p. 22 © Bettmann/Corbis; p. 28 Stock Montage, Inc.

Library of Congress Cataloging-in-Publication Data

Tecco, Betsy Dru.
  How to draw the life and times of Grover Cleveland / Betsy Dru Tecco.— 1st ed.
      p. cm. — (A kid's guide to drawing the presidents of the United States of America)
  Includes index.
  ISBN 1-4042-2999-X (library binding)
  1. Cleveland, Grover, 1837–1908—Juvenile literature. 2. Presidents—United States—Biography—Juvenile literature. I. Title. II. Series.

E697.T43 2006
973.8'5'092—dc22

                                2004027028

Manufactured in the United States of America

Contents

Young Grover Cleveland

Stephen Grover Cleveland was both the twenty-second and the twenty-fourth president of the United States. He was born on March 18, 1837, in Caldwell, New Jersey. He was the fifth of nine children born to Richard and Ann Neal Cleveland. His father was minister of the First Presbyterian Church in Caldwell.  Cleveland was named for the church's earlier minister, Reverend Stephen Grover. Some of his childhood friends called him Big Steve because he was a large boy, but he liked the name Grover.

As a minister's son, Cleveland grew up in a religious home. His father was well liked by church members, and his mother helped those who were poor or sick. The Clevelands taught their children that success in life was measured by good behavior, hard work, and honesty.

Grover Cleveland was a good student, but he was not the best in his class. He studied hard to earn good grades. At the age of nine, Grover wrote an essay that explained why time should never be wasted. "If we expect to become great and good men and be respected and esteemed by our friends, we must improve our time when we are young," he wrote. Grover Cleveland was not lazy. As president of the United States, he tried for a while to do everything himself. He even answered the White House telephone instead of hiring a secretary. Cleveland frequently stayed up well past midnight working. He had a job to do, and he planned to get it done.

You will need the following supplies to draw the life and times of Grover Cleveland:

✓ A sketch pad   ✓ An eraser   ✓ A pencil   ✓ A ruler

These are some of the shapes and drawing terms you need to know:

Horizontal Line	—	Squiggly Line	
Oval		Trapezoid	
Rectangle		Triangle	
Shading		Vertical Line	
Slanted Line		Wavy Line	

Rise to Fame

Grover Cleveland's rise to the presidency came early in his career. He went from being mayor of Buffalo, to governor of New York, to president of the United States in only three and a half years. He was known to be a hard worker and an honest man who believed in justice for all people. As both mayor and governor, Cleveland improved government by stopping corruption, or dishonesty, among politicians.

As the twenty-second and twenty-fourth president, Cleveland was the only U.S. president elected to serve two terms that were not one after the other. Benjamin Harrison, the twenty-third president, served one term between Cleveland's terms in office. Cleveland's first term began in 1885. Cleveland was the first Democrat in 28 years elected to be president. The Democrats had become unpopular because of their support of the Southern states during the Civil War. Cleveland's victory over the Republican candidate, James G. Blaine, marked the Democrats' return to national popularity.

One year after Grover Cleveland became president for the first time, he made history by becoming the first president to marry in the White House. On June 2, 1886, he married Frances Clara Folsom in the White House's Blue Room.

Pathway of the Revolution

Grover Cleveland Park is a state park in Caldwell, New Jersey. Located near Cleveland's birthplace, the park has a lake, tennis courts, and several walking trails.

New Jersey

Map of the United States of America

Grover Cleveland is the only U.S. president to have been born in New Jersey. New Jersey is known as the Pathway of the Revolution, because more than 100 battles were fought there during the American Revolution. One of the 13 original states, New Jersey entered the Union in 1787.

Cleveland was born in the tiny New Jersey village of Caldwell. It was named in 1798 in honor of James Caldwell, who was a minister who supported General George Washington during the Revolution. The house where Cleveland was born is now a museum. Officially called the Grover

Cleveland Birthplace State Historic Site, it is the only house museum in the country that honors President Cleveland's life. His birthplace has the most complete collection of Cleveland artifacts in the nation.

Cleveland returned to his home state in 1897, when he retired to Princeton, New Jersey. That same year Cleveland received an honorary degree from Princeton University. In 1901, he was named a trustee of Princeton. After Cleveland died in 1908, a small funeral was held. President Theodore Roosevelt was one of the few people to attend the simple service. Cleveland was buried in the family plot in Princeton Cemetery. His name appears on the gravestone, but it says nothing about the fact that he was president of the United States, because Cleveland did not want any special honors.

Grover Cleveland is one of the more famous people to be buried in Princeton Cemetery. Cleveland's wife and daughter Ruth are buried on either side of him.

Boyhood Jobs

The house where Cleveland was born was built in 1832. It was the manse, or pastor's residence, for the First Presbyterian Church at Caldwell. Cleveland's father was the minister here from 1834 to 1841. Today most of the first-floor rooms are the same as they were in 1837, the year Cleveland was born.

When Cleveland turned four, his family moved to Fayetteville, New York. He had fun playing outdoors. His favorite activity was fishing, which he would enjoy his entire life. Cleveland received a good education at Fayetteville Academy. He looked back on his years at Fayetteville as a very happy time in his life. However, his father did not make much money, so Cleveland and his brothers had to find jobs after school.

In 1850, the family moved to Clinton, New York. Cleveland had to leave school at the age of 14 in order to help support his family. He worked for two years as a store clerk. He lived in a cold room above the general store with another clerk.

1 You are now going to draw the house where Cleveland was born. Begin by drawing a large rectangle that is slanted. Draw more slanted lines to form another rectangle beside it. Add lines on the right side.

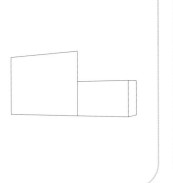

2 Draw lines to form the top of a triangle. Draw the lines below the triangular top. Add the shape above the two shapes on the right. Draw a line across the two slanted rectangles. Add a slanted line to the bottom right.

3 Erase any extra lines. Add slanted lines to the roof, creating pointed shapes. Draw a horizontal line and a rectangle in the main part. Add lines to the side section of the building. Include the ones behind it.

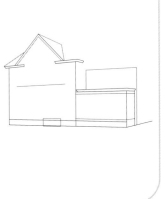

4 Erase extra lines. Draw a chimney and add two roofs. Add windows and a door. Add lines for the side of the step area below the door. Add a horizontal line and a few vertical lines to the side part.

5 Erase extra lines. Draw the side of the chimney you drew in step 4. Add another tall chimney. Add sides to both parts of the building. Add more windows. Add details to the door and porch. Add steps.

6 Erase extra lines. Add lines to the sides of the roofs and chimney as shown. Add details to the front window. Add more windows to the building. Add details to the entrance and the porch. Draw bushes at the front.

7 Erase extra lines. Looking carefully at the drawing and the picture on the opposite page, add as much detail as you would like. Finish with shading. Notice which parts are darker than others.

Studying the Law

Grover Cleveland was 16 when his family moved to Holland Patent, New York. Cleveland's father died on October 1, 1853, within weeks of the move. His death ended Cleveland's hopes of attending college. More than ever it was necessary for him to continue to provide for his family. Cleveland took a job as an assistant teacher at the New York Institution for the Blind in New York City.

At age 18, Cleveland decided to leave for Ohio with hopes of studying to become a lawyer. On the way he visited an uncle, Lewis F. Allen, in Buffalo, shown above. He convinced Cleveland to stay in Buffalo. He found Cleveland a job as an apprentice clerk at the law firm of Rodgers, Bowen and Rodgers. Cleveland worked long hours on the job and studied law. In May 1859, he passed the New York State bar exam and became a lawyer at the age of 22. His new job at the law office earned Cleveland $1,000 per year. A few years later, as president of the United States, his salary would jump to $50,000 per year.

1

You are going to draw a boat taken from the scene in Buffalo, New York, on the opposite page. Start by drawing a curvy line for the water. Add more lines for the base of the boat as shown.

2

Draw a long curving line above the shape you have just drawn. Draw two small vertical lines connecting it to the base of the boat. Draw horizontal and vertical lines to create three rectangles. These will be small cabins.

3

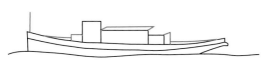

Draw a vertical line at the left side of the boat. This is a flagpole. Draw two lines next to the rectangle on the left. Draw a slightly curving line that connects to those new lines. Add more straight lines to the rectangles you drew in step 3. Draw another curved line on the right side of the boat.

4

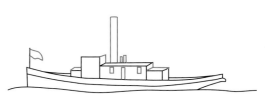

Add the flag to the flagpole. Add more straight lines to the cabins. Draw three chimneys on top of the longest cabin. See how one of the chimneys is large and tall, and the other two are quite small. Add two windows and a door as shown.

5

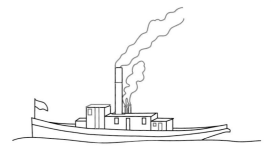

Finish off the roof of the cabin on the left. Add vertical lines and a window as shown. Add lines to finish the chimneys, including the smoke that is blowing from them. Add a window and a door to the cabin on the right.

6

Erase extra lines. You can finish your drawing with shading. Make the shading lighter in some areas as shown. Well done. You have finished your picture of the boat.

Entry into Politics

When the Civil War began in 1861, Cleveland was already a successful lawyer. Rather than join the army, he chose to continue his career. His mother and younger sisters still needed the money he gave them. He was also interested in politics and joined the Democratic Party. His first government job came in 1863, when he was made assistant district attorney of Erie County. Then from 1871 to 1873, he served as Erie County's sheriff.

Cleveland then returned to his law practice for a few years. In 1881, he was elected mayor of Buffalo. Wanting to make changes that would improve how the city government was run, Cleveland vetoed, or turned down, so many laws that wasted public money that he became known as the veto mayor.

In 1883, Cleveland became governor of New York. That year the Brooklyn Bridge was completed. Shown above is Governor Cleveland leading the first walk across the bridge.

1

Begin by drawing a large rectangle. Draw a smaller rectangle inside it. Draw a vertical line down the middle of the rectangles. These will be your guides to drawing the Brooklyn Bridge.

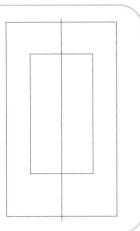

2

Draw the two pointed arches within the inside rectangle. Draw three small lines to make a trapezoid on top of this rectangle, which is separated by the vertical line. Add four slanted lines that extend to the large rectangle.

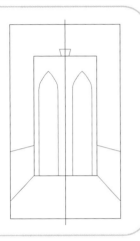

3

Add two more slanted lines. Add shapes to the top of the trapezoid. Draw a column on either side of the bridge. The columns have trapezoids at the tops. Draw a horizontal line between the columns. Add the shapes above the arches.

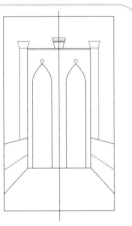

4

Add lines to the tops of the columns as shown. Draw small vertical lines in the trapezoid in the center. Draw another column on either side as shown.

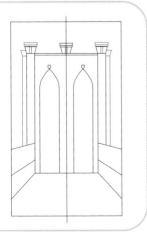

5

Add lines to the new columns. Draw four sets of cables that slope down from the top of the bridge. Add the three horizontal lines at the top. Draw two more slanted lines, one on each side.

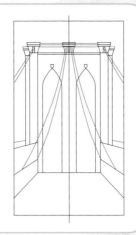

6

Erase the center guideline. Erase any extra lines. Draw many curved lines around the cable lines. See how the cables in the center are bigger than the ones on the side. Draw vertical lines coming from the side cables.

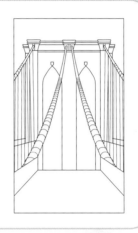

7

Look at the drawing and the picture on the opposite page to help you add details to the bridge. Finish your drawing with shading. Well done!

A Dirty Campaign

FOR PRESIDENT.
GROVER CLEVELAND
of NEW YORK.

For VICE PRESIDENT.
THOS·A·HENDRICKS
of INDIANA.

While he was governor of New York, Grover Cleveland once again fought against wasteful spending. As a result Cleveland was chosen as the Democratic candidate in the presidential election of 1884. His campaign poster is shown here. He had proven that he was an honorable man who wanted to get rid of cheating politicians.

The campaign, however, was one of the dirtiest in American history. Ugly stories were spread about both candidates. James Blaine, the Republican candidate, was accused of corruption. Cleveland was accused of being the father of an unwed woman's child. The claim did not seriously hurt Cleveland's campaign because he handled the matter honestly. On Election Day Americans voted for Cleveland, who beat Blaine by 25,685 votes. Some of the votes for Cleveland came from a group of Republicans called mugwumps. The mugwumps were tired of wrongdoing in their own political party and wanted an honest government.

1 You are going to draw the eagle and flag that are on the Cleveland poster. Draw a long, slanted shape for the flagpole. See how it is thinner at the top. Draw an oval around the middle of the pole, with the curved shape coming out from the side of it.

2 Erase the extra lines. Add the shapes for the eagle's beak, chin, and one of its wings. Add a circle to the top of the flagpole. Draw a curved line toward the end of the flagpole and add the shape at the bottom of it.

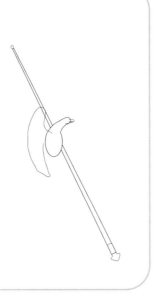

3 Erase extra lines. Add feathers to the wing. Draw the top of another wing. Add lines to the head. Draw lines coming from the beak. One of the lines goes all the way to the top of the pole. Draw the shape at the top of the pole. Add lines to the bottom of the pole.

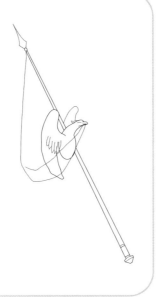

4 Erase extra lines. Add more feathers to the wing in front. Finish the other wing. Finish the eagle's eye. Draw another line coming from its beak. Draw the line as shown until it meets the wing. Add lines to the flag. Add details to the top and bottom of the flagpole.

5 Draw stars on the flag. Notice where some of the stars are partly hidden by the folds in the cloth and by the eagle's wing. Add more folds in the flag as shown.

6 Erase any extra lines. You can finish your drawing with shading. Make sure to leave the stars white, though. Well done! You have finished drawing the U.S. flag and the eagle, which is a symbol, or sign, of the United States.

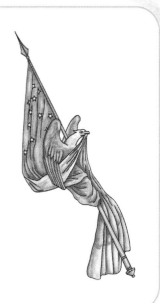

First Presidency

When Grover Cleveland came to office, the federal government had plenty of money. However, the new president saw that the money was being spent on unnecessary projects. To stop the wasteful spending, Cleveland turned down more than 300 laws. He became the "veto president." He refused hundreds of pension claims because they were false. Many of the people who applied for the pensions lied about their war service. He also fired government workers who were unnecessary or unable to do their jobs well.

Cleveland's job was not all about vetos and firings. On October 28, 1886, Cleveland publicly accepted the Statue of Liberty, which was a gift from the people of France. The invitation to the event is shown above.

One of the most important bills Cleveland signed was the Interstate Commerce Act in 1887. For many years railroads could charge passengers and shippers whatever they liked. Often the rates were unfairly high. The Interstate Commerce Act made sure that the railroads charged "reasonable and just rates."

1 Now it's time to draw the Statue of Liberty. Draw a rectangle. Use a ruler to draw a long vertical line going through the rectangle's center. Next draw a horizontal line that crosses the vertical line.

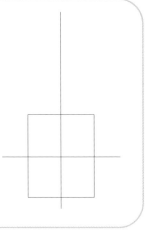

2 Draw two horizontal lines across the rectangular guide. Draw more lines to form two rectangles on top of the top line you just drew. Next draw an oval as shown. This is your guide for Lady Liberty.

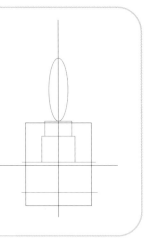

3 Slightly off center of the vertical guide, draw an oval for the head. Add guides for the face. Draw guidelines for the arms and ovals for the hands. Add more straight lines to the statue's base.

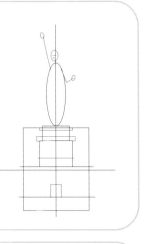

4 Add the face, hair, and neck. Using the guides draw her arms and hands. Draw the paper she holds. Add straight lines and rectangles to the top half of the base. Draw the shapes as they appear in the bottom half.

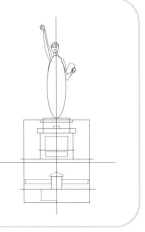

5 Erase the face, arm, and hand guidelines. Add more details to her head and use the guides to draw the dress. Begin to draw the torch in her extended arm. Draw her fingers. Add details to the base.

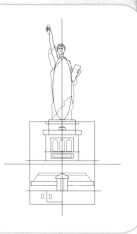

6 Erase the guidelines. Erase any extra lines. Finish the torch. Draw her hair and add spikes to the top of her head. Add her thumb. Add folds in her dress. Add more details to the base.

7 Erase the rest of the guidelines. Looking carefully at the drawing and the picture on the opposite page, add as much detail to your drawing as you would like. That's it. You're done.

Love and Marriage

Grover Cleveland was 47 and single when he first became president. He surprised the nation in 1886, when he announced he would marry Frances Folsom later that year. Only 21 years old, Frances was the daughter of his former law partner. Her father had died when she was 11, and Cleveland was put in charge of her care. By the time Frances graduated from Wells College in Aurora, New York, in 1885, Cleveland had fallen in love with her. The wedding took place at the White House on June 2, 1886. Only about 30 guests attended the event, but the entire nation was interested in the marriage because Cleveland had been a bachelor for so long. Frances was the youngest First Lady in U.S. history. She charmed Americans with her gracious manner.

The Clevelands had a strong marriage. They had five children, three girls and two boys. Their first child, Ruth, was so adored by the nation that the candy bar Baby Ruth was named after her.

1

Begin your picture of Cleveland's wife, Frances, by drawing a large oval. Draw a bent line coming from the oval. Next draw three slanting lines that cross over each other as shown.

2

Inside the oval draw lines for the eyes, nose, and mouth. Draw small ovals for the ears on either side. Draw curved lines for the jawline. Draw the outline of the neck and arms around the body guides.

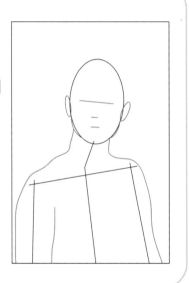

3

Erase the body guides and any extra lines around the jawline. Add the hair and the ears around the guides as shown. Add the eyes, eyebrows, nose, and mouth. Draw the collar around the neck area as shown.

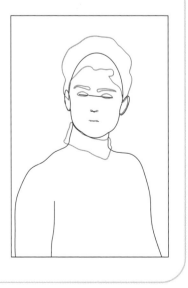

4

Erase extra lines. Add circles inside the eyes and lines around the mouth and nose. Add details to the ear. Draw the squiggly lines on the collar for the pin. Draw outlines for the shoulders and arms. Add lines to the front of the dress.

5

Erase extra lines. Draw squiggly lines to add curls to the hair. Add curved lines for the eyelids. Add details inside the eye circles. Add lines to the mouth and chin areas. Finish the pin. Draw the folds in the dress.

6

Erase extra lines. You can finish your drawing with shading. Look carefully at the drawing and try to copy the shadows as they appear on Frances's face. Shade in the background, too. Well done!

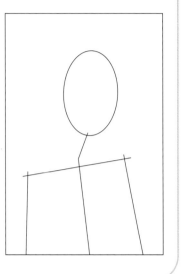

1888 Campaign

By 1887, the federal treasury had $103 million more than the government needed to meet its yearly expenses. Cleveland proposed lowering tariffs, which were fees charged on goods from other countries. He believed that the

high tariffs gave the government money it did not need. Many disagreed, and Cleveland lost popularity.

In 1888, Cleveland ran for reelection. The Republican Party chose Benjamin Harrison as their candidate. He was the grandson of William Henry Harrison, the ninth U.S. president. Because Benjamin Harrison favored high tariffs, Cleveland lost many votes to him. American businesses thought high tariffs helped them compete against businesses in foreign countries. In November Harrison won the presidency.

As president, Harrison passed a new tariff that raised rates higher than ever before. Congress spent so much money during Harrison's term that the U.S. Treasury was almost empty by the next presidential campaign. Cleveland was angry and decided to run again.

1 You are now going to draw the rooster. The rooster was a symbol, or sign, of the Democratic Party. Start by drawing a large oval that is slightly tipped. Draw a circle that crosses over the oval. Add the curvy shape above the circle.

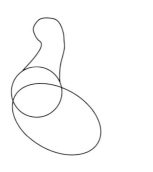

2 Draw the pointed shape for the beak. Draw a large wavy line for the start of the tail. Draw the legs. See where they cross over the bottom part of the oval. Draw the shape as shown for the perch.

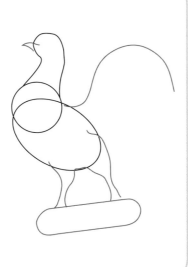

3 Erase parts of the oval and circle guides as shown. Draw the lower part of the beak. Draw a circle for part of the eye. Add curvy lines to the tail. Draw two curved lines for the front of the body. Draw two claws.

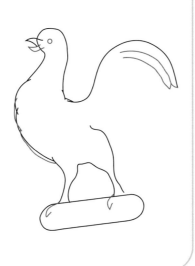

4 Erase extra lines. Draw the eyelid and add the shape below the beak. Add more feathers to the tail. Draw a large curved line for the wing. Add more claws to the rooster's feet. These help him balance on the perch.

5 Erase extra lines. Add the squiggly shape, called the comb, on the top of the head. Add the shape below the beak called the wattle. Draw two curved lines in the neck. Add more tail feathers. Draw feathers on his legs.

6 Looking carefully at the picture, add the faint lines to show the feathers all over the cock's body. You can finish your drawing with shading. Notice where the shading is darker in some parts than in others.

A Second Term

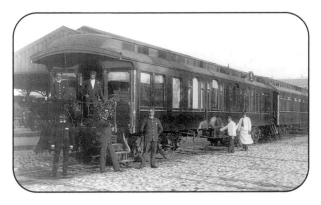

In 1892, Cleveland beat Harrison. His second term, however, was not easy. Two months after he took office, the United States experienced its worst economic depression yet. Fifteen thousand businesses failed, and four million people lost their jobs. Cleveland thought the problem was having both silver and gold for the nation's currency because people had traded their cheap silver coins for expensive gold coins that they saved. This drained the federal reserve of its gold supply, causing hundreds of banks to fail. Cleveland convinced Congress to base the nation's currency solely on gold. Unfortunately, his efforts did not solve the shaky financial situation.

Cleveland's popularity was further hurt when the Pullman railroad company in Illinois cut jobs and pay. On May 10, 1894, its workers went on strike. Trains carrying Pullman railroad cars, like the ones shown here, were burned and taken apart by angry workers. Cleveland decided the strike was a federal crime and sent 12,000 troops to stop the protest. People across the country thought he had acted too severely.

1

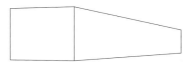

Begin by drawing a rectangle that is at a slight angle. Draw a long shape at the right side of the rectangle. See how it becomes thinner at the end.

2

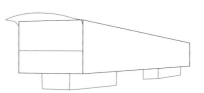

Draw the curved roof at the top of the rectangle. Draw a horizontal line inside the rectangle. Draw shapes as shown underneath the train.

3

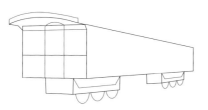

Add a curved line to the roof. Draw another horizontal line in the front section. Add the door. Draw half circles for wheels and add lines to the box shapes you drew in step 2.

4

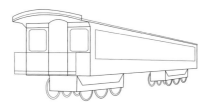

Erase extra lines. Draw the line that goes all along the top. Draw windows in the front. Add the rectangle with the horizontal line inside it. Draw the slanted rectangle at the side and add more wheels. Add lines to the wheels you already drew in step 3.

5

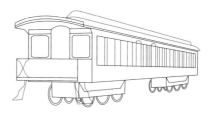

Erase extra lines. Draw the shape at the top of the train. Add straight lines for windows along the side. Draw two curved lines above the middle section of the windows. Add a rough X to the front. Add more details to the front as shown.

6

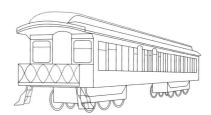

Erase extra lines. Finish off the roof by adding the curved line at the top. Draw horizontal lines at the tops of some windows. Draw four more rough X shapes. Add more details to the front.

7

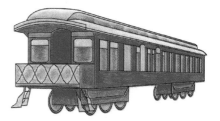

You can finish your drawing with shading. Some parts are shaded in darker than others. Well done! You have finished.

An Unpopular End

By the second half of his second term in office, Grover Cleveland became so disliked that he ordered the White House gates locked to keep out angry Americans. As the depression continued into 1896, Americans felt Cleveland was unable to solve the country's troubles. In fact they blamed him for most of their problems. He lost his fight for lower tariffs and he failed to help Americans who were poor and out of work. When he left the White House in 1897, Cleveland realized people no longer believed he could do the job. He did not run in the next election because the Democrats chose William Jennings Bryan as their candidate instead.

In 1897, Grover Cleveland retired to a 15-acre (6 ha) estate in Princeton, New Jersey, shown here. He happily worked on the board of trustees and as a lecturer, or teacher, at Princeton University from 1901 until his death. His greatest joy, however, was his family. After years of working long hours, Cleveland finally took time to relax with his wife and children.

1 You are going to draw the home in Princeton where Cleveland retired. Start by drawing a small rectangle. Draw the large, slanted shape beside it. These will be your guides.

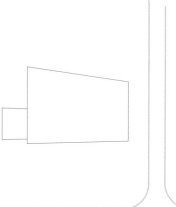

2 Add lines to the small rectangle. Draw the side wall on the left that peaks at the roof. To start the roof, add lines going across the top of the main section. Draw a new, smaller section on the right side.

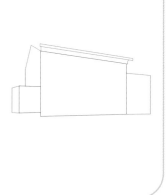

3 Draw vertical lines in the small rectangle. Looking carefully at the drawing, draw all the straight, curved, and slanted lines along the top of the house, including the side section. Add a rectangle to the front.

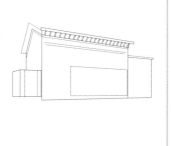

4 Add details to the main roof. Draw lines in the section on the left. Add a window. Add more lines to the rectangle in the main section for a porch. Draw a chimney on the roof of the right side. Add a rectangle.

5 Erase extra lines. Add shutters to the window. Add details to the chimneys, the side of the main roof, the porch, and the shape on the right. Draw squiggly lines on the left section. Add more windows.

6 Erase extra lines. Add more windows and shutters. Add more details to the chimneys on both roofs. Draw steps at the front porch. Draw a bush at the right side. Add the remaining lines to all three sections.

7 Erase extra lines. Finish the chimneys. Add details to the windows. Add the doorway and more windows at the front. Add details to the porch. Add a doorway at the right side. Add more steps and add another bush.

8 Look carefully at the drawing and the photograph on the opposite page, and add as much detail as you would like. You can finish your drawing with shading. Well done! That was a hard one.

Honest and Earnest

Throughout his political career, Cleveland was an honest, fair, and practical man. These qualities served him well as a lawyer, sheriff, mayor, governor, and president. He lived at a time in America's history when corruption was common. Yet Cleveland believed that "a public office is a public trust." He was able to bring back confidence, or belief, in the government by standing up to dishonest people. Even though he made enemies with his unbending ways, Cleveland stuck to what he believed to be true and right.

Grover Cleveland failed to overcome many of the challenges he faced as president, but he is respected today for his strength and honesty. Known as Good Grover, Cleveland always considered what was best for the people, not for himself. As president he took his job of serving the country very seriously and never misused his power for his own personal gain. On June 24, 1908, Cleveland died with his wife by his side. His last words before he died were, "I have tried so hard to do right."

1

You are now going to draw a portrait, or picture, of Grover Cleveland. Start by drawing an oval. This will be your head guide. Draw a line coming from the oval. Next draw two slanting lines that cross over each other as shown. These will be your body guides.

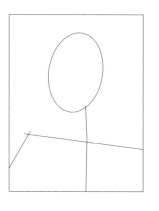

2

Draw three lines across the face guide. These are your guides for drawing the eyes, nose, and mouth. Draw a small oval at the side for an ear. Draw a curved line above the ear oval for the side of the head. Draw wavy lines on either side for the neck and shoulders.

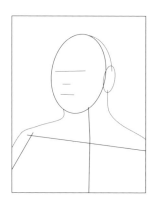

3

Erase extra lines. Next draw the eyebrows, eyes, and nose. Draw a rough line along the side of his face. Draw a squiggly line for Cleveland's chin. Using the ear guide, draw the ear. Draw the neck line coming from the ear as shown.

4

Erase extra lines. Draw his hair. Add more lines to the ear. Add circles and lines to the eyes as shown. Add more lines to the nose and draw the mustache. Draw the lines for his jacket and shirt collar. Begin to draw his tie.

5

Draw more hair at the top of his head. Add lines to the hair you drew in step 4. Finish the insides of his eyes and ear. Add mouth lines and a chin line. Add a curved line to his neck. Finish his tie. Finish his jacket. Don't forget the button!

6

Erase extra lines. Add details to his hair and mustache as shown. You can now finish with shading. You can shade in the background if you like, too. See where the shading is darker in some parts. Well done! You did a super job.

Timeline

1837 Grover Cleveland is born in Caldwell, New Jersey, on March 18.

1853 Cleveland's father dies, leaving him to support the family.

1855 Cleveland studies law in Buffalo, New York.

1859 Cleveland passes the New York State bar exam to become a lawyer.

1863 Cleveland is appointed assistant district attorney of Erie County.

1865 Cleveland is beaten in the election for Erie County district attorney.

1870 Cleveland is elected sheriff of Erie County. He serves for three years before returning to his law career.

1873 Cleveland becomes a member of the firm Bass, Cleveland, and Bissell.

1881 Cleveland is elected mayor of Buffalo, New York.

1883 Cleveland is elected governor of New York.

1884 Cleveland is elected twenty-second president of the United States.

1886 Cleveland marries Frances Clara Folsom in the White House.

1888 Cleveland loses reelection to Benjamin Harrison.

1892 Cleveland is elected twenty-fourth U.S. president, beating Harrison.

1893 Businesses close as depression begins. Cleveland has an operation for mouth cancer.

1897 Cleveland retires in Princeton, New Jersey.

1901 Cleveland is elected trustee of Princeton University.

1908 Cleveland dies on June 24 and is buried at Princeton Cemetery.

Glossary

American Revolution (uh-MER-uh-ken reh-vuh-LOO-shun) Battles that soldiers from the colonies fought against Britain for freedom, from 1775 to 1783.

apprentice (uh-PREN-tis) Having to do with a person who learns a trade by working for someone who is already trained.

artifacts (AR-tih-fakts) Objects created and produced by people.

bachelor (BACH-lur) A man who has not married.

Civil War (SIH-vul WOR) The war fought between the Northern and the Southern states of America from 1861 to 1865.

currency (KUR-en-see) Money.

Democrat (DEH-muh-krat) A person who belongs to the Democratic Party, one of the two major political parties in the United States.

depression (dih-PREH-shun) A period during which business activities are very slow and many people are out of work.

essay (EH-say) A short piece of writing written from a personal point of view.

esteemed (ih-STEEMD) Thought highly of.

foreign (FOR-in) Outside one's own country.

honorary degree (AH-neh-rer-ree duh-GREE) A rank or title given by a college or a university as an honor.

institution (in-stih-TOO-shun) An organization that is set up for a special purpose.

lawyer (LOY-er) Someone who gives advice about the law.

pension (PEN-shun) Money paid when a person retires from a job.

Republican (rih-PUH-blih-ken) Referring to one of the two major political parties in the United States.

residence (REH-zih-dens) A place to live.

site (SYT) The place where a certain event happens.

strike (STRYK) A refusal to work until changes are made.

trustee (trus-TEE) Someone who is put in charge of something.

Union (YOON-yun) Another name for the United States.

vetoed (VEE-tohd) Did not allow laws proposed by another department or branch of government.

Index

Web Sites

Due to the changing nature of Internet links, PowerKids Press has developed an online list of Web sites related to the subject of this book. This site is updated regularly. Please use this link to access the list:
www.powerkidslinks.com/kgdpusa/cleveland/